You Are Rich

Wes Lee

Published by Wes Lee, 2020.

YOU ARE RICH

First edition. August 27, 2020.

Written by Wes Lee.

Also by Wes Lee

Impactful Leadership

You Have A Purpose

You Are Free

You Are Successful

Professional Persuasion

The Brave Bunch (Children's Book)

Watch for more at amazon.com/author/wes_lee

I dedicate this book to you. Your commitment to getting rich inspires me.

TABLE OF CONTENTS

INTRODUCTION

If there's anything that dramatically influences the level of success of anyone, it's mindset and behavior towards wealth and prosperity. Everything that manifests in your life has a subconscious backing. A thought comes before every action; you can't create wealth if you're not programmed to *think* wealth. One of the glaring and significant differences between a rich man and a poor man is often their behavior and subconscious mindset towards wealth.

Thinking wealthy is the very first step on this rollercoaster ride. Still, a vibrant mind isn't enough to create a change in your physical world, without actions. You are blessed to be alive and have your dynamic brain. Not taking these significant measures to build wealth is equal to throwing away your blessing. Another distinguishing characteristic of the rich and the poor is the ability to *do*. While the productive "do," the unproductive talk.

To successfully "do," you need a strategy. The steps you take in your actions and the approach you use are the last vital piece of the whole. If this piece is missing, you'll continuously go in circles, get overwhelmed, frustrated, and quit (we've all been there at least once). Your success strategy's a vital sign-post on your road map.

You are RICH, and all that matters is your Mind, Actions, and Success Strategies. MASS. A weighty mass will always occupy space and make a significant difference.

Let's get it!

By the end of this book, you'll know:

- How to control your mind to produce anything you want

- The importance of a wealthy mindset

- How to reprogram your mind and the necessary tools needed

- How what we see, hear, and say determines our brain's programming

- The *actions* essential to your success

- What you need to stop doing to achieve

- How to maximize your production with no extra time

- Why the right success strategy is important

- How to engineer your custom success strategy

- Some practical and collective approaches to take advantage of

- How to live the MASS principles

- Why you can't focus on your mind alone, without applying productive actions and a success strategy

PART I: YOUR RICH MIND

CHAPTER ONE: MIND CONTROL

"You can only control two things in your life: Your attitude and your actions." Darren Hardy

The ability to feel stems from the mind. The mind's often referred to as the seat of consciousness and thought, the very place of our cognitive awareness and imagination. The power and importance of the brain are absolute. Your mind controls your physical expressions, manifestations, and actions. Logical deduction says that the ability to control our mind will cause a radical change in the wellness and effectiveness of anyone.

Here's a classic example of the mind's potent influence on our success and well-being. Have you ever heard of the PLACEBO effect? A placebo effect is a fake treatment believed to be real. Doctors track patients for changes in behavior such as elevated moods and more energy. The doctor assures the patient that they'll improve. The patients' mind subconsciously believes a lie, which becomes their reality. When patients start to feel better, they get pumped up and excited about this improvement. The improvement tricks them into believing the fake drug works. Their strengthened belief, more often than not, increases the effect of the treatment until they feel cured.

Your *intention* is a robust tool that can take on a life of its own to effect radical change. Understanding that the subconscious mind controls the expression of the physical is crucial to determining your success. Thinking with *intention* is not just hypothetical. It is more than just a seat of consciousness; it is the power that drives action, will, and grit.

The subconscious mind is the sum of what we see, hear, say, and believe. Think of it like food. Some people feed their minds with "candy," others fill themselves with "apples." These people aren't totally to blame, because it comes from their

6

childhood. Imagine a child that grew up in a family who eats two meals a day. It's typical for that child to be subconsciously satisfied with two meals a day. They *see* it as being normal; why would they change? What we see and experience shackles or elevates us.

While we're the expression of what we see, you should know that the mind's also influenced by what you say and hear. Ultimately, we're the ones that control our mind; we control what enters the brain and how it functions. We are the god of our thought process, our consciousness, and our imagination, the controllers of our minds.

Chapter Summary/Key Takeaways

In the next chapter, you'll learn and understand the underlying thought process we all go through. Now that you know that we control our thought and what goes into our minds, you will learn how to direct and channel your thinking into getting results.

CHAPTER TWO: HOW WE THINK

"What you focus on expands." T. Harv Eker

Our thinking has a framework controlled by the brain. We can think, and we can *unthink*. You need to know the thinking framework and how to harness it for your benefit.

Thinking is the use of our cognitive ability to process information, solve life problems, take actions, and generate new ideas. Thought disorder is a mental illness that affects the way people think. People with thought disorders can't put together a belief in the right sequence. Can you imagine the difficulty this causes? The ability to *think* and *think properly* is vital.

Our minds become programmed through our thinking. Thoughts get influenced by sight, hearing, and feeling. Even when you imagine something that doesn't exist, your past thoughts fuel it. Our belief system is consistent with our previous ideas, which programs our minds. I explained how the brain controls *meaning* in the physical, the *result* we experience, and what we *see*. If your thought process is the key to unlocking your mind, then you need to learn how to improve it.

When we focus on a particular idea, it starts to take different forms and materializes in our imagination. We think in a cascade of events where one event leads to another, and another. The sequence of these events, however, isn't definite. It is more like we are always on a road that forks into several different routes. In our thoughts, we choose a path, and in that path, choose another way. But sometimes, our mind may not be strong enough to take a route. Have you ever locked onto a problem you can't solve? Your brain needed to grow to the level of that problem. But don't forget that this chain always starts with *input* from the past or present.

To strengthen your thoughts and access new parts of your mind, do this.

1. THINK OFTEN: Jean Lamarck's law of "Use and disuse" applies to how our thinking process improves. Many may argue that we think every day, but there's a difference between everyday thinking, critical thinking, and creative thinking. We use our brains to think in four ways, Divergent, Convergent, Critical, and Creative. The first two are the rational thinking process we employ every day. However, weeks and months can pass before using Creative and Critical thinking. Creative thinking is the process where we generate new ideas. Critical thinking refers to the careful and analytical study of something to form a judgment. If you use this thought process regularly, you will discover how easy it becomes for you to develop opinions and nurture creative ideas. It's your power whenever you want it.

2. THINK POSITIVE: The key to your mind is the emotions you choose to feed. If you're always thinking negatively, then you'll program yourself in a limiting and negative way. You won't access positive thoughts when you need them, which will kill growth, self-development, and goals. Positive thinking creates strength and grit in your actions; negative thinking steals it away.

3. READ: You're already doing it! The benefit of reading is that you're limitless. Reading opens you up to ideas, strengthens your imagination, and takes you beyond yourself. Studies show that the best workout for your brain is reading. It will help to keep the cognitive ability of your mind stimulated. Also, reading helps increase memory strength, which you need to succeed.

Read often, and you will notice a revolutionary change in your thoughts and results.

Chapter Summary/Key Takeaways

In the next chapter, you'll reprogram your mind and supercharge your thoughts. So far, you learned the brain's essence, how it controls all that we are, and how our thoughts determine our programming. Next, you'll learn how to use this thought process and other tools to reprogram yourself and get lasting results.

CHAPTER THREE:

REPROGRAMMING YOUR MIND

"I can do all things through him who strengthens me."
(Philippians 4:13 ESV)

Our minds programming determines the actions we take, our beliefs, and our results. In the first chapter, you saw a typical example of a limiting mindset. Now, you'll learn how to reprogram your mind and crank out results. Nature wants you to prosper, but first, you need to start from an abundant mindset.

The way to our mind is via three channels: what we see, what we hear, and what we say. If any of these three are defective, then our mindset is broken. I'll explain how these three affect the way we think.

WHAT WE SEE

What we see determines the richness of our minds. In the first chapter, I told you about a child that grew up eating two meals a day. If the child doesn't know any other reality than the one he sees, he'll believe that eating two meals a day is typical; what he sees becomes his belief. What if his environment changes? What if he gets exposed to a culture where people eat more than two meals a day? The new environment will make him question his belief in eating twice a day. Slowly, he'll change because he reprogrammed himself to accept a new idea.

Can you see how sight determines our mind's programming? To reprogram your mind, change the meaning of what you *see*, choose to make it suit your desires. If you want to build a car company, surround yourself with pictures of cars and successful car companies, *look* at them every day. How can you change your environment? Do something (anything) different! For most people, their environment limits their mindset. But you are not most people! Where you place yourself, determines what you will regularly see. If your surroundings are toxic to your growth, change your setting.

If your dream and vision aren't near you, travel. Travel to Paris to look at beautiful structures if you want to be a real estate mogul. Where is the life you want? Surround yourself with your visions again and again. You can surround yourself with them by a book, the internet, and travel. Don't accept your mind if it tells you, "I can't afford that," or "I can't do that!" That thinking will give you a life of things you can't afford or can't do. All because of the *belief.* Instead, ask yourself, "*how* can I have that?" or "*how* can I do that?" When you surround yourself with your desires, you discover that your brain's receptive to accept your new thoughts, the same ideas that seemed impossible before. In essence, what you *see* affects what you can *do*. People detest the news because of the bad press they *see*. Who has ever watched the news and felt empowered to conquer the world? Nobody. Your only barrier is how you think and what you accept as the truth.

Another way to reprogram your mind is through perspective. The news has constant disasters, should that deter you from pursuing what you want? Never! Instead, take it as a challenge to be different and stand out. Unleash your unique mindset, try something new, and prove your old-self wrong. Change your perspective when you see things you don't agree with and watch your life flourish.

WHAT WE HEAR

If what you hear's always negative, your life will take a negative turn. If what you hear's positive, you'll profit. The gateway to the mind isn't just our eyes, but our ears too. People will have wrong opinions about you. Some will have no encouraging words, and you may discover that you're continually struggling with self-esteem and self-belief. What you hear is significant to your *belief* in yourself. Some people regularly talk about how difficult it is to survive in the world. Others talk about how hard it is to stand out. Some will even complain about how impossible it is to enter the Forbe's list. Your mind becomes limited, narrowed, and restrained when you hear this *little* talk. Hear it enough, and you start to believe it! And in no time, their beliefs become yours. *Listening* works the same as *seeing,* which is especially true with the news. The news feeds weak mindsets. The press spread the <u>false</u> impression that people need to be *informed.* People indeed need information; however, people need the information that empowers, not frightens.

If you want to be free from the pressure you've placed on yourself, by *hearing* the wrong information, you must start listening to those that are where you want to be. Listen to content from people with no limits in life. Follow free podcasts with rich messages. Surround yourself with people that show you new possibilities. *Decide* that you create your reality, that you can do anything you want (because you can!). Reprogram your mind and self-esteem; your faith in self-actualization will increase.

All your life, have you been used to people telling you that you're not capable? It's time to find that minority that says you are!

WHAT YOU SAY

What we say is a reflection of our inner world. You're about to see how what we *say* can reprogram our minds.

What we *say* is an expression of what we *believe.* Remember the placebo effect? When a patient does a placebo treatment, the doctors take an audio report of the patient's health. In a situation where the patient responds positively to the procedure, the patient (from time to time) tells the doctor that

14

they feel much better. These self-affirmations and confessions get repeated again and again, leading the patient to *believe* they're improving. We are *whatever* we say we are.

If you wake up every morning and tell yourself, "I'm mad," a person who continues this for a few days is likely to wake up one day and be mad. This example is to show you that what we say feeds us positively (apples) or negatively (candy). Re-affirming what you want to be, has a strong effect on your belief system. Use this to reprogram every negative in your mind with a positive. What new story can you tell yourself, and what negative words need to turn positive in your life?

Next, *listen* to things that tell you what you want to be, but don't flatter yourself, *saying* and *hearing* positive words is an empty practice, without <u>action</u>. When you begin to "do," you experience the success you crave. You'll see results when you <u>work</u> for them (action). But, naturally, an abundant mind already wants to "do" because of its programming. Many people don't want to work for their success; the proof's in the "lottery mindset" that millions of people have. They believe that winning the lottery will solve all of their problems. They dream of a $10 ticket, making them a multi-millionaire. These are the people that are happy to throw away hundreds of dollars to win a $10 scratch-off. Focused action (work) in the right direction sets more people free than the mega-millions jackpot.

Chapter Summary/Key Takeaways

In the next chapter, you'll learn the importance of taking focused actions. You already discovered how to reprogram your mind, but that's only one of the factors required for success. Results won't occur without work (action).

PART II: YOUR RICH ACTIONS

CHAPTER FOUR: WHY OUR

ACTIONS ARE IMPORTANT

"Each step you take reveals a new Horizon..." Dan Poynter

The actions we take determines what we believe. You can't claim that you aim to be among the richest in the world while waking up late in the morning every day. Our actions show our conviction, tenacity, extent, and the lengths we'll go to see that we get what we want.

The actions we take are essential to how we express ourselves. It's the final tip to the iceberg; a wealthy mindset can't get you where you want without the necessary steps. Having a *vibrant* mind and *weak* action is like business professors who choose to *teach* when they fail in the business world. These professors are intellectual but hide in the classroom to avoid practicing (taking action on) what they teach. Can you see why you need to take action, and it needs to be *productive* action?

"Our actions determine our destiny" is a trendy phrase. All the actions we take are the sum of where we eventually arrive. The steps we take have three categories. They are:

- ⯀ Daily actions

- ⯀ Planned activities; and,

- ⯀ Inspired actions

1. Daily actions: We take specific measures every day that support us and move us towards our goals. What do you always execute at a particular time of the day? For many, it's a workout regimen. Or what activities do you

17

consistently perform at a given time? When actions become habits, we don't think about them anymore; they're effortless. The benefit of daily habits is that they deliver structure and routine in our day. They're also a way to invest in our future, compounding our efforts to get a result. Exercising every day, over time, adds up to a healthy physique. Doesn't it? Our Daily Habits add fuel to the fire and keep us ready for almost anything, especially setbacks. There are daily habits that are proven to improve our target achievement. Some include visualizing goals, saying affirmations, meditating, reading, and exercising. These disciplines will help us achieve goals by effectively handling stress, controlling focus, sustaining energy, and motivating. Operating from your best state serves your ideas and opportunities. When we improve our decisions, we get what we want. You're tapping into the motivation you need to act on your plans and achieve.

2. Planned Actions: Planned actions are the specific actions we take when we need to accomplish something. They're the actions we take to achieve (they are conscious actions). Planned activities are decisions that we make from drafting an action plan for our goal. Sticking to your plan moves you towards the outcome you want. For example, if you're going to complete a marathon six months from now, create a schedule of distances you plan to run every week and every day. That run is your scheduled course of action. Or, if you want to start a new business, define the steps that you plan to take over the next 90 days (or longer). Planned actions are different from daily activities because we perform these actions with goals in mind. Daily activities also have reasons backing them up. Still, the purpose of everyday activities relates to essential needs, such as survival (eating food and drinking water).

3. Inspired Actions: Inspired actions are how we respond to inspiration or an idea; they're intuitive. We can find solutions to problems we're facing or generate a fabulous string of creative ideas. These solutions and insights appear from nowhere (because we're following daily habits). If you have an idea, don't wait, take action! What can you do today that will move you closer to that idea? You probably won't find these actions on your action plan initially. Instead, these will be special instructions that you receive from a higher place of knowledge. Inspired activities can help or hurt depending on the situation; your ability to decide will determine your outcome.

Chapter Summary/Key Takeaways

In the next chapter, you'll learn how to strengthen the results you get from your actions. You've seen in this chapter how the richness of our activities determines the outcome. You've also learned the type of prosperous behavior to adopt. In the next section, you'll learn how to maximize your actions and get more positive results.

CHAPTER FIVE: MAXIMIZE YOUR

ACTIONS

"It is better to take many small steps in the right directions than to make a great leap forward only to stumble backward" Chinese Proverb

The actions we take have to be productive to work. Our daily activities, planned actions, and inspired actions have to be aligned to see results. In this chapter, you'll learn how to maximize your production and create effective results.

DAILY ACTIONS

As you know, daily actions are the actions we take that become routine. Every day a rich person performs work differently than the average. You need to behave like the person you want to be, not the person you were yesterday. Many people want to be one way, but don't *act* it every day. Don't think you need to *achieve* something first, to be a certain way. You don't need to be wealthy, to *act* wealthy. Daily activities become habits, which become your identity. If your daily actions aren't productive, your potential for success is low. These daily habits will enrich you.

1. Practice waking up earlier than you used to: One of the daily actions that show a productive mindset is your response to time. Time is gold. Don't give more than 8 hours of your day to sleep and expect a significant change in your life. Warren Buffet and Jeff Bezos attest to the fact that they sleep a *maximum* of 8 hours every day. This Sleep schedule produces results for established people that are incredibly well-developed. To get what

20

you want, you'll sacrifice more hours of sleep. But aren't your goals worth it? However, rest is still critical to your sanity; you could (in the name of success) sleep 2 hours daily. Yet, your effectiveness and productivity will tank, then your actions will suffer. Laze in bed a little bit, daydream about what you want, but get enough sleep for your brain to function correctly.

2. Practice saying daily affirmations: I already explained in the earlier part of this book the importance of an abundant mindset. A wealthy mindset will create productive action. Speaking what you believe every day, will reprogram your subconscious mind to align with your goals. To say it is to think about it. Your thinking produces strength, will, and grit. You can surf the net for daily affirmations that align with what you want or craft your own. One of mine is, "I am a champion; I am changing this world; I am fearless, I am limitless!" Examples of others are, "money comes to me; I am a magnet for money." Or "It's easy for me to succeed; profit is easy." Speak your new beliefs every morning or before you go to bed (I prefer morning).

3. Make sure to read every day: Reading is one of the best ways to learn when you're not doing. Reading is crucial and life-changing because you only need to connect with one idea to change your future. I'm so glad you're here with me reading this! There's reading material for everything you want to experience. Unlike most people, read with a conscious *purpose*. Learn about wealthy people, read books of value. I've included a vetted book list at the end of this book just for you. Make sure you read meaningful content every day; fill your mind with fruit, not sugar. Mark Cuban spends about 3 hours a day reading, and attributes books to the secret of his success; Bill Gates and Mark Zuckerberg read for hours also. Elon Musk said that when he was in grade school, he

consumed books for at least 10 hours a day. One of the attributes that most billionaires practice and employ daily is their voracious habit of devouring profitable books. If there is any sure way your mind can reprogram, it's by reading with intention.

PLANNED ACTIONS

Planned actions are the intentional actions you take because you have a goal. Planned activities are for the sole purpose of getting you closer to what you want. These planned actions have three processes.

1. Semantic Process: The first part of our planned actions is the semantic process, which involves the mind. It's in this stage we utilize our mind and conclude what will benefit us and bring the ultimate positive result. Use the combined effect of desire, a positive mindset, and all of your resources available to make a firm decision about the steps you want to take (be gritty and scrappy). Before you choose any stage for your planned actions, write the pros, cons, and net benefits. Don't waste your time pursuing the end of a circular rope. It's essential that you effectively use the semantic process before taking any planned action.

2. The training process: This is the stage you learn to affect your decisions, especially if the actions you decided are unfamiliar. Read up on the steps you want to take and build yourself slowly until you excel. If I want to improve my skills in advertising, I'm going to pay for the training to do it. Are you willing to make education your highest monthly expense? If you are, you won't destroy your time and money to opportunity costs. If I invested in training for $2,000, would it be worth it to avoid losing $10,000 on my mistakes with Ads?

22

Absolutely! Education's an infinite return that no one can take from you.

3. Life Task: Your planned actions take full effect and determine your results. It's a life task because you can't afford to take the wrong step. Your planned activities are the actual steps you take towards realizing your goals. In contrast, you can lose progress by making avoidable mistakes; it's costly and time-consuming to make mistakes that you can avoid.

To be successful, own your mistakes. There's no one to blame, except ourselves. This mindset is wealthy because self-accountability is rare. We're our only obstacle. Whatever achievement you have will happen because you made it happen, which also goes for failure. Other people aren't responsible for your success, so they can't be accountable for your setbacks. Realize this when you take the wrong step because it happens to us all. Acknowledge mistakes, retrace your actions, and keep flowing forward.

Your success strategy comes from your planned actions. If your planned activities don't take you towards your goals, review them. Don't try to run east, thinking you'll see the sunset.

INSPIRED ACTIONS

Your inspired actions are the actions you take when you reach a crossroads. We make thousands of different decisions every day (we even decide to make a decision). Many are easy, but others are complex, stressful, or both. Because there are many decisions (forks in the road), it impacts results, costs, time, effectiveness, feelings, and relationships. How you make your decisions is vital. Decision making is a top priority when facing a challenge because you're choosing a road, successful or not.

Below are the things to do when you reach a "fork" and need to make a choice.

1.   Consider the overall benefit of the decision you want to take. Weigh the risks of both paths and determine which one has a better effect. Often, we're faced with a severe decision-making problem when things don't go as planned. We need to be aware of other decisions we can use as alternatives to the original plan. It's crucial to weigh the risks that can arise from your choices.

2.   What are the pros of your alternative decisions? Just like it's essential to weigh the decision with the least disadvantages, it's crucial to make choices with more advantages.

3.   Is not taking any action an alternative? Can it bring better results than all the other options you have? Sometimes, we think we need to change our path when things seem to turn bad, but you may be only an inch from getting what you want. It's been my experience that the hardest challenges come just before the most significant breakthroughs.

Chapter Summary/Key Takeaways

You know how to maximize your actions, daily activities, planned actions, and inspired actions. Using these tools is essential. In the next chapter, you'll learn critical success strategies, and why it's crucial, you have them.

PART III: YOUR SUCCESS

STRATEGY

CHAPTER SEVEN: WHY THE

SUCCESS STRATEGY IS

IMPORTANT

"A vision without [a] strategy remains an Illusion" Lee Bolman

A success strategy refers to the plan you make that provides you with guidance, ordering your steps to success. It's the method you employ to make your goals materialize. Your success strategy doesn't refer to your business plan. Still, it can be a part of it, as I mentioned earlier. I'm referring to the set of choices we make to *eat the elephant*. Your success strategy helps to focus your decision making because you have guidelines. A plan keeps you in your "success lane" on the fast track.

If you don't have a successful strategy, then you only have visions without values. Your success strategy is the *value* system for the goals you have, and it helps you measure your goals. It's almost impossible to track your progress if you don't *measure* it.

Strategic planning's vital because it's the planning for the *whole* enterprise, not bits and parts; it's the forest, not the trees. It's not the same as business planning, however. Strategic planning needs to decide and shape the business plan; it's not production planning, though it guides production. It's also not a type of workforce, technology, or any other kind of partial planning. It's not marketing, even if it guides who and where to market. It's not a matter of planning, forecasting, or budgeting. It's a system designed to produce a business strategy, a list of objectives to ensure you're achieving over the long-term.

Here are some benefits of having a successful strategy:

1. Planning: While a successful strategy isn't a form of planning, it supports your action plan. Your success strategy helps you have a clearer picture of what you want to do and sets a guideline for you to plan your steps.

2. Strength and Weakness: Your success strategy helps you leverage your strengths and find the weaknesses you have. Your success strategy helps you see your limitations so that you can do something about them. Don't waste time and money working on your weaknesses; it's terrible advice. What do you do? Build a network of people who are *strong* where you're *weak*. At the time of this writing, I'm also publishing a children's picture book. But I don't draw. So, I've surrounded myself with top-notch illustrators. What's the point of learning to draw for 15 years (working on my weakness) when I can hire someone? Would I be saving money, learning to do it myself? No. I'd lose more than the illustrator costs, in book royalties, over 15 years. Most universities force people to work on their weaknesses, but it's pointless and frustrating.

   On the other hand, are you exploiting your strengths? Are you trying to close skill gaps (vulnerabilities) in your business plan? Use your strategy to creates greater awareness of yourself, focus on the elements that will make you successful (strengths), and find people who close your gaps (weaknesses). Don't try to do everything yourself. You'll lose time, money, and it doesn't work.

3. Resource Pool: Your success strategy allows you to see the resources available to you. You have resources, unique abilities that only you can employ. Those skills are your unfair advantage to thrust you to the next level.

Recognizing your resources helps you maximize your strengths. You can't use what you don't know you have.

When considering a success strategy, there are some specific questions to ask yourself.

- What are your beliefs and core values?

- If you're a product or service business, what market do you serve?

- What's the range of products you want to offer, and how profitable is each?

- What's your financial capability?

- How will you sell your idea?

Chapter Summary/Key Takeaways

In this chapter, you'll understand the success strategies you can use today. You'll also see and learn useful tactics. You've already learned the benefit of having a successful plan and the questions to form your strategy around.

CHAPTER EIGHT: YOUR SUCCESS

STRATEGY

"Strategy without process is a little more than a wish list" Robert Fliek

Success strategies always depend on what you want. My plan to reach goals is different from everyone else. Our approach may be similar, but it will be different because I'm not you.

You know yourself best, and you know your capabilities. What strategy will work best for you? There are strategies that *everyone* should use, no matter the goal; these are unavoidable. I'll list out what will get you results.

START SMALL

No matter what business plan, life goals, or self-achievement you want, it's essential, you start small. Starting small is a training process; you learn the nuances and complexities of your success plan. Relay runners don't learn to be the best in a day, and you can't hit the gym once and be fit for life. We all need to put in the time consistently. You wouldn't set a goal to go to the gym to throw out your back, would you? Never! But how many people "throw out their back" in other areas of their life? They don't want to build up themselves over time; they want to start at the end. *Patience* is one of the biggest reasons people quit and don't get what they want. They're trying to *get it* overnight.

No one gets rich overnight, except the lottery, and that's not a financial plan. But what about Mark Zuckerberg? He got rich overnight! Kylie Jenner got rich overnight, right? Just like other outliers, there are many things behind the curtain that you didn't see. That "overnight" success was the release of *pressure*

29

from many years of build-up (work). You won't lose 20 pounds in a day, but you can lose one pound a day till you crush your goal. This success strategy works for all purposes and guides you in your decisions.

BE CONSISTENT

One of the best ways to strategize is consistency; you can't try a method today and expect it to be there tomorrow. Consistency is the key to hard-earned success (grit). This strategy is tailor-made with starting small. What's responsible for the lack of progress is a lack of consistency in taking action. Impatience causes people to deter from plans right before a breakthrough.

Consistency teaches you new ways you're doing things wrong. It shows you (with experience) how to do it right. It forces you to show up every day, making success your way of life. Consistent action, no matter how small, has more power than you can imagine. If you took nothing from this book, except to *show up for life every day*, you'd get what you want.

ALLOW FOR SETBACKS

Nothing hits people harder than setbacks. Setbacks are frustrating, but there's no gift more excellent than *failure*. Every billionaire is a person that faced delays in life. However, they come out differently because they're willing to fail more than others. They go after goals and seek failure, understanding that it's just part of the game. They understand that setbacks and perseverance will hand them whatever they want. The beautiful story of Thomas Edison is a widespread one. While most people see failure as a setback, he chose to see the breakdowns as a gift, an avenue of learning. When he was asked, "How did it feel to fail a thousand times?" he said, "I didn't fail 1,000 times. The light bulb was an invention with 1000 steps."

When you meet setbacks, as part of your success strategy, look for ways to overcome and persevere. A prosperous mind will know what it wants and will do whatever it takes to reach it.

EMPLOY THE SWOT ANALYSIS

SWOT analysis is a productive and effective success strategy. SWOT analysis is not only applied to business, but it's also for your personal life because *you are your own business*. SWOT stands for four elements, Strength, Weakness, Opportunity, and Threat. Your job is to examine these four elements in your success plan. You want to know your strengths (the things you can do). Your "strengths" refer to your unfair advantages over others. What unique traits do you have? What's easy for you, that others find hard? Leverage them, because you're always at your best when you're living in your strengths. Your weaknesses relate to everything you do that reduces your effectiveness (I'm not great at math). Any trait that serves to "weigh you down" is a weakness. Strengths and weaknesses are intrinsic (internal factors) to SWOT analysis. Logically, you want to put strengths in your asset column. Also, you want to *acknowledge* your weaknesses. Don't waste time trying to improve your weaknesses, acknowledge they exist, and decide how you'll get past them. There's always someone else in the world who excels where you're *weak*. Give your weaknesses to them.

The extrinsic (external factors) of SWOT analysis are Opportunities and Threats. Opportunities refer to the available resources that you can harness to create an unfair advantage. Threats apply to the unfair advantages that others can use against you. Continually use SWOT analysis to recognize your opportunities faster and pair them with your strengths. Think of it as a process that's alive. Use SWOT to realize where you're weak so that you can surround yourself with people who have that strength. Also, monitor your threats, so that you have responses for your risks.

Here's how this plays out. I'm going to invest in the stock market because I have attention to detail (strength). However, I'm not great at math to calculate my breakeven point (weakness). I'm liquid $100,000, and stocks are on sale (opportunity). But, I don't have any *control* over the S&P 500 (threat).

I analyze my potential trades carefully (strength) and use an online calculator to figure out my breakeven (compensating for weakness). I've figured out that the stock only needs to move $1.50 for me to profit (opportunity). I protect my trades -against risk- with put options, in case the stock drops (acknowledging threats and managing risk). This process grows as you grow, use it regularly, harness your strengths and opportunities, and flourish.

EPILOGUE/CONCLUSION

Your mind is luxurious and elegant enough to affect the result you desire. We're all equipped with the necessary tools to skyrocket us to wealth; it all boils down to our Mind, our Actions, and our Success Strategy. Apply these tools, get results, and live the quality of life you deserve.

Positive and substantial change comes by applying "*MASS.*" Reprogramming your mind to a rich one isn't enough to create a significant difference unless you take action. And, your actions can't produce results unless you use the right success strategy.

You're precious; your mind is vibrant, and your actions are productive, make a difference, and use your gifts!

P.S. I want to give you a bonus chapter from my co-authored book, *Impactful Leadership*.

Would you leave a review for this book? Your thoughts are precious to me.

I appreciate you and look forward to your success stories!

With love, Wes

BONUS: CHAPTER 1 OF

IMPACTFUL LEADERSHIP

Discovering Your Leadership Style

What is Leadership?

The best place to begin our journey is with an understanding of effective leadership and why we make the decisions we make. The most effective leaders create permanent change and transform lives with their actions.

Leadership is a learned skill, and everybody can be an impactful leader. Everyone is a leader, from parents who want to impact their children to volunteers who hunger to contribute to their community. Any person who wants to be a beacon of light for people can lead, and every day is overflowing with opportunities to rise to your potential!

As we begin this exciting journey together, we'll dive into a new way of viewing leadership that I've learned and put into practice for years. This book celebrates the phenomenal work performed in human needs psychology trademarked by Tony

Robbins. For our purpose, leadership will focus on our ability to influence other people by discovering what already influences their behaviors, emotions, actions, thoughts, and feelings.

I want you to visualize yourself, making a tremendous impact on people. You can imagine a single person, a group of people, your team members at work, or anyone in your life whom you want to influence. What if you had the skills to take people you and move them to achieve outstanding results in their lives and change for the greater good? How fulfilled would you feel to shift these people and know that you lead them to exceptional results?

For the past ten years, I've been on a mission to grow and introduce success into every fiber of people's lives. In my quest, I wrote a best-selling course that's reached 40 countries and counting. And, I've worked with some of the most elite fortune 500 companies, in industries from real estate to technology. What I can say confidently is that we all have habits that are at the core of who we are.

When you learn to apply these timeless principles into your own life, you'll equip yourself to transform your quality of life. You'll lead other people to shift their thinking, the way they feel, actions they take, and ultimately their life. And your ability to move people is your mark as a leader. Let's Begin!

HUMAN NEEDS PSYCHOLOGY™

Developed by Tony Robbins and refined by Cloé Madanes: Human Needs Psychology™ is a discipline focused on the absolute needs that each of us shares as human beings. It doesn't matter if a person is a radical, royalty, homeless, middle class, black, white, red, orange, sick or healthy, young or old. We'll utilize this psychology as the base to propel your ability to lead and make massive progress with yourself and others. Sound great? The goal of this discipline is to uncover new choices, behaviors, actions, thoughts, and feelings that a person may not have known they have within them. We'll impact people in ways that feel good to them, and help them meet their deepest needs, by introducing new and enlightening ways to get what they desire.

How do we Make Decisions?

Life doesn't "happen" to us. We create our lives, and it's our decisions that shape our lives. So, how do we make decisions that create our lives? We're making three decisions every second of every day, which affect us in the interim and over the long term.

How are you using your body? Such as your breathing, how tall you sit or stand, and how you move.

Where's your focus? What you're focused on is what you feel at any moment.

Did you notice that 1 & 2 are non-verbal? The third factor is: what words do we assign to an experience? The language we assign to an experience determines how we feel. If you say: "That makes me <u>mad</u>!" you're right, and you'll feel it. If you say: "That makes me <u>happy,</u>" you're also right, and you'll also feel it.

When we're in distress or pain, it's because we're inwardly focused. And one or all of the above three factors are off. The fantastic part is that you're in control of all three! And the more robust these three factors are, the more significant you'll feel. You'll also make more empowering or less empowering decisions.

Example

If someone's having difficulty, you can focus on the problem or be the solution. Ask yourself, "how can I contribute to this person right now?"

Pay attention to the language you use, and that other people use. We can use enhanced or diminutive language. Let's say someone asks you, "How's your day?" you can choose to respond: "Good," or you can enhance your language and say, "Phenomenal." Do you think you'll feel different depending on how you respond? Or let's say you or another person encounters a tough situation. Does it "Suck" or is it "Inconvenient." You're using diminutive language, adopting a style that's less harsh and negative.

Lastly, the quickest way to instantly affect your mood at any given moment is to change how you use your body by changing your physiology. If you or another person is sitting, stand up. If you feel down, take deep breaths. Go for a walk, stretch out, or pay attention to the foods and drinks you put into your body that day. These all positively affect your body and your state, which enables you to be more effective in making significant decisions.

How we Shape Our World

It's no secret that each of us is unique and superior in certain aspects of life. We're also inferior in other dimensions, making us all even. Now, you already understand the three decisions we're making every second, that affect us in the interim (short term). Next are the factors that affect our life over a long period. How we perceive the world, what it means to us, and how it affects our decisions.

Each of us is After Six Human Necessities:

1. We want to feel certain

2. We want variety and a sense of change

3. We all want to feel like we matter

4. We want to experience love and feel connected

5. We each want to feel as though we're growing

6. We want to think that we are contributing to something beyond ourselves

Each of us Has a Map to Guide us to our Desired Necessities

1. We have universal beliefs about the way life is

2. We each have desires and fears

3. We each have methods we rely on to meet our necessities

4. We all have boundaries for ourselves (Thresholds)

5. We have situations in which we would violate our thresholds

6. We have a belief system about who we are

7. We all have preferences in how we make decisions Ex: (Big Picture vs. Detail-oriented)

Each of us Has Emotions we Default to

These emotions can be emotions that give us strength or make us weaker. Reflect on yourself for a moment; what are your go-to feelings? When I was growing up, I lived in an emotional frame of anger. If I didn't like something, I'd get angry. Even If something happened that I wanted, sometimes I'd get mad because I wouldn't feel worthy of that kind gesture. So, where do you go to often within yourself?

Six Human Necessities

What's fascinating is that we meet these necessities in ways that help us and harm us. Every person has a way to meet these necessities, however. As leaders, we want to discover how a person is getting their needs met. We need to influence them to achieve their needs in ways that are pleasurable and positive over the long term of their life. Make sense? So why do you think a person would do something harmful such as drink or do drugs? Why do addictions even happen? I used to believe it was the drug itself (which plays a factor!). However, an enlightening moment occurred for me when I realized that it has more to do with *us* than the outside stimulus. People in my family had drug problems, and wisdom taught me that the drugs were meeting several of their necessities. If that drug meets enough needs, it creates an addiction. What are the three essential needs a drug addict wants? Write three of the six.

1.

2.

3.

We're each unique in the way we value these necessities. Every person is different and meets these in different ways. You'll know your essential needs in a stressful experience. We tend to value a couple of these needs over the others; however, we still require all six. So, which two showed up for you the last time you experienced a challenging situation? For me: I value growing, and I appreciate the feeling of significance. I get anxious when I feel like I'm not growing, and I highly value feeling like I matter. The combination of those necessities is why you're reading this material.

Our Guiding Map

Are you meeting your needs?

How do you know if you are?

What do you believe?

What thresholds have you placed on yourself to achieve your necessities?

Your Default Emotions

Do you remember the last time you expressed an emotion quicker than you could think? We act on our feelings, which positively or negatively affect our quality of life.

Recap

Ask yourself these three questions throughout

the day:

1. What meaning do I choose to give this situation?

2. What action am I going to take?

3. What do I choose to focus on right now?

Understanding Yourself First

Before leading other people, it's critical to know how you perceive the world and how your perspective interacts with another person's view of the world. Expanding your understanding of yourself brings you the ability to develop your influence and knowledge of other people, giving your life more options and flexibility.

If you want to impact anyone and shift their perspective to make positive changes, you have to understand what already motivates them. We can't effectively change a person for our reasons. Leadership means understanding how they see the world and how you can help them meet their necessities for their purposes.

Have you ever had someone tell you all of the reasons why you should change? Did you resist changing? Unless you were after the same necessities as that person, you probably resisted it because they didn't understand how you see the world.

How Happiness Works

Do you know why you get upset or frustrated, and why you feel ecstatic in certain parts of your life? When I learned and applied this, it was mind-blowing and straightforward! There are two factors we can shift to achieve happiness and take ourselves out of a painful state of being:

1. We have the control to change our situation

2. We have the power to change the narratives in our mind

Example

My wife and I, at the time of this writing, live in Hawaii. I highlight this because this is the most fulfilling area of my life. It's the most fulfilling area because our marriage exceeds my perception of marriage. I always imagined marrying my best friend, what I never envisioned was living in such a beautiful place and making life into a wondrous adventure! So, because my marriage exceeds what I imagined, I'm thrilled! Now, let's look at the other side of this. When I was a teenager, I didn't have money, and I didn't have a relationship or a place of my own to live. My situations (Relationship, Finances, and Living) didn't match how I perceived things should be. In my mind, I wanted lots of money, a great relationship, and a beautiful place to call mine. Because I had none of those, what could I have done? I could have changed my situation and started aggressively going after what I wanted. Or I could have changed the way I perceived being single, with no income or a place of my own. I could have said, "I'm working on myself, so I can have everything I desire." Instead of "I'm not worthy of having the things I desire," Can you see the power in this small shift? Change the situation or change the way you perceive the situation.

Action Steps

1. Where are you thrilled in your life right now? What pleases you about it the most? Pay attention and write down IF your expectations meet or exceed the situation.

2. What area of your life do you want to improve in the most? What doesn't please you about it? Do your expectations meet how you imagine it should be? How can you use this information to change it?

3. What are your top two human necessities of the six? Take ownership of them. Think of them as your best friends, and feel proud because they are your primary drivers (Think about which necessities you live and embody each day).

RECOMMENDED READING LIST

- *Impactful Leadership* by Wes Lee

Impactful Leadership:
amazon.com/author/wes_lee

- *Secrets Of The Millionaire Mind* by T. Harv Eker

- *Millionaire Success Habits* by Dean Graziosi

- *The Success Principles* by Jack Canfield

- *Think and Grow Rich* by Napoleon Hill

- *The Richest Man in Babylon* by George S. Clason

- *The Power of Broke* by Daymond John

- *Principles* by Ray Dalio

NEXT STEPS

Also by Wes Lee

Impactful Leadership

You Have A Purpose

You Are Free

You Are Successful

Professional Persuasion

The Brave Bunch (Children's Book)

Read more at amazon.com/author/wes_lee

About the Author

Wes Lee is a passionate advocate for success with over a decade of experience and a business degree from Hawaii Pacific University. Best known for his Leadership in the Army and operating multiple successful businesses, including lending money in 42 states, starting a business that significantly reduces health-care costs, and taking ownership in a life insurance company. Lee's books take his hard-won experience and translate it into easy recipes you can follow to achieve massive breakthroughs. His site https://twitter.com/wes_lee_success shares strategies and resources to have everything you want from life while getting paid handsomely. Wes loves living in Kapolei, Hawaii (a personal dream) with his wife and digging his toes in the sand at the lagoons of Ko'olina.

Follow at
https://www.tiktok.com/@weslee1988

www.ingramcontent.com/pod-product-compliance
Lightning Source LLC
Chambersburg PA
CBHW031500210526
45463CB00003B/1006